KITCHEN

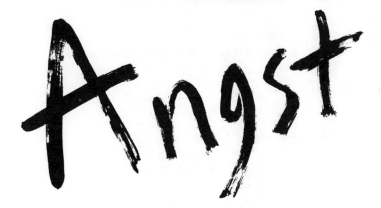

Have You Got Problems?
Cook 'em Out

Margaret Sullivan (signature)   *17 September 1993*

Margaret Sullivan

Designed by Rebecca Binks

CHICAGO REVIEW PRESS

For Norman and Anthony and X

Library of Congress Cataloging-in-Publication Data

Sullivan, Margaret.
    Kitchen angst: have you got problems? cook 'em out / Margaret
Sullivan.—1st ed.
        p.   cm.
    Includes index.
    ISBN 1-55652-196-0 : $11.95
    1. Cookery.   2. Cookery—Humor.   I. Title
TX714.S84 1993
641.5'0207—dc20   93-3713
                                                    CIP

Verso page designs by Rebecca Binks

©1993 by Margaret Sullivan

Published by Chicago Review Press, Incorporated
814 North Franklin Street
Chicago, IL 60610

Printed in the United States of America

ISBN 1-55652-196-0

5   4   3   2   1

Angst

Henceforward burn what thou hast worshipped,
and worship what thou hast burned.

St. Remy
438-533 A.D.

The Recipes

MEATS, POULTRY, AND FISH

SANDWICHES, EGGS, AND PASTA

VEGETABLES

DESSERTS

INDEX

Angst

NONE OF THE RECIPES HAVE BEEN TESTED
ON LABORATORY ANIMALS.

Angst

I would like to thank everyone in the entire world except the people who said they would help me with this and didn't.

I would also like to withhold thanks from those who strove to sabotage these efforts, whether it was ruining my child-care schedule, walking off in the middle of a job, trying to make me feel guilty about how bad their lives are, or otherwise assuming that anything matters more than food and the need to prepare it.

Really, what I mean is:

Thank you

Jeanne Giles, Gayle Mitchell, Hanna Takashige, Angela Hricsina, Alton Miller, Audrey Kissel, Paui Dillon, Peter Taub, Robert Dubiel, Cary Donham, Cindy Stockman, Thomas Lopez, Ayn McClain.

Angst

RECIPE FOR A DYSFUNCTIONAL KITCHEN

2 tons of bitter sarcasm
1 sorry bag of resentment
10 lbs. of frustration

Several sets of useless and embarrassing cooking implements:

Cheap wobbly knives
Yellow plastic measuring cups
Blue potholder with ducks
A toaster oven

Shake it all up and toss in a lifetime of constant betrayal and low self-esteem.

Angst

YIELDS SCHMIELDS

These recipes describe productions that should serve four people under "normal" conditions. An example of an abnormal condition is cooking to resolve failed romantic events, in which case, despite the amount of food you create, the recipe should serve only one, and should be eaten in the closet.

Angst

A Total Philosophy of Kitchen Angst Via an Appendix of Inflexible Rules

1. Cooking is the resolution of pain and frustration. It is not about pleasing others or creating some hysterical and temporary "warmth" or friendliness. Because it involves intense concentration, some yelling and destructive thoughts about others, Kitchen Angst cooking is best done alone.

2. Paper napkins peel apart, make food and paper combinations stick to your fingers, remind one of toilet paper, and suggest that they came free with something. You should use them only in the movie theater, in which case you deserve to suffer because you get to go out.

3. People who measure things don't eat sugar or meat, nor do they allow their children to watch television. They need to be treated for obsessive-compulsive disorders. Nature presents food in piles, and it should be measured as such.

Pile of spices (actual size)

4. While it is unstoppable that most people prefer to socialize in the kitchen, that doesn't mean they should ever be allowed to touch anything.

5. Kitchen Angst cooking transcends all time and allows you to vindicate those with whom you did battle far into the past. Their packaging represents the standard for hyperactive decoration and personal expression. You must therefore select them on that basis and bow down to their pretensions.

6. Olive oil and wine are high involvement purchases. Their

7. If it moves, eat it; i.e. don't overcook anything, especially meat, unless you resent your dining companions.

8. The world is your kitchen. You may remove anything at any time from your world as long as it graces your kitchen.

Elements of a Perfect Existence

Virtually noiseless

Virtually dishless

Impossible to ruin

Can be used as a love potion

Can be used as a protective spell

Has color therapeutic value

Can be eaten in the bathtub

Can be made in bed

DREAM JOURNAL

I am at a formal party near the water cannon on the Chicago River. I look exactly like the queen of a small nation in a gold and white striped sarong dress and emerald sandals. My nails are painted white. Just when I'm in the heart of a perfect moment, I notice that all the women at the party are wearing my clothes, stolen from my closet, or should I say given to them by my boyfriend. My boyfriend has taken all my dresses and given them to these other women. Holy Balls.

A Rather Private Snapper Soup

Food

- ½ pound snapper
- ½ cup olive oil
- 1 cup flour
- Several small scallions, chopped
- 2 pureed tomatoes or 1 cup canned
- 1 clove garlic, crushed

- 2 bay leaves
- 1 teaspoon cloves
- 1 teaspoon allspice
- 1 teaspoon parsley
- 2 cups water
- 2 cups chianti or other red wine
- 1 cup port

Action

Don't ever let anyone watch you make this soup. No one is that trustworthy. People who have recently ended relationships with you will try to beckon your replacements to cook this for them. Worse still, your exes may attempt to make this themselves, which is somehow a stronger betrayal. Oh sure, they can steal your clothes in your nightmares, but they can't take a recipe that's locked in your daydreams.

Start with the cleaned and prepared snapper. All you want to do is make this magnificent gravy in which you cook the fish, then slowly thin the creation with water, wine, and port until it is soup. Just brown the oil and flour, then the scallions. Next come the tomatoes and garlic. Let that settle in over low heat for 5 minutes. Now come the bay leaves, cloves, allspice, and parsley. This is what you fry the snapper in, turning it once. Then alternate 1 cup of liquid every 10 minutes like this: water, wine, port, water, wine—low heat all the while.

3

THE ACADEMY FOR WEALTHY SOCIALISTS

Dear Professor Angst:

This will confirm your appointment to join our faculty in the Department of Liberal Education. Your new course:

The Metaphysics of Cooking

promises to be very popular.

Observe that, contrary to your handbook, you are not entitled to insurance benefits or the use of the gym. Also, please remember that faculty washrooms are for tenured faculty only.

Eventually, perhaps after a few semesters, some of the other faculty may wish to meet you.

Good luck.

Yours sincerely,

The Dean's Office

Potato Soup to Tide You Over Until You're Wealthy and Important

Food

- 6 tablespoons butter
- 3 leeks, sliced
- 8 red potatoes, sliced
- 3 cups chicken stock
- 3 cups milk and half-and-half combination, depending on how much your heart can take

- ½ teaspoon mace
- Salt and white pepper to taste
- Handful parsley, chopped

Action

Melt the butter and sauté the leeks and potatoes until soft. Pour in the stock and milk mixture (all at once is fine); add the mace, salt, and pepper. Let it simmer quietly for 10 minutes before you add the parsley. Ten minutes is plenty of time for you to reflect on how much you and this soup have in common: it's so cheap, and you're so unappreciated; it's so elegant, so are you; it's about to be crushed by a machine. Now you should pour all this into a blender or food processor; otherwise you must anguish in the disgusting business of pressing it through a strainer. Then return it to the pan to heat until serving. You might garnish with the more attractive bits of unused parsley.

5

My special friend **angst**,

Just writing to share the wonderful news that I have returned from Bali, where I have been designing exciting fashions and teaching peace and understanding to those who think peace matters.

I'm back now with a hundred tender stories about real people who care, and a hundred new designs. Won't you come to my opening reception and show?

Remember to keep your smoking escorts at home!

Yours for real,
agnés
(Say AHN-YAY)

Corn Chowder: What to Make When Life Hands You Corn

Food

- 2 tablespoons each butter and olive oil
- Black and red pepper to taste
- 6 ears of corn, sliced away from the cob
- 1 clove garlic, crushed
- 2 tomatoes
- 2 pounds shrimp or clams
- Water as needed

Action

Just pile it in (the way some people pile it on). If you find the process of removing corn indelicate, or perhaps too violent, I guess you can use canned or frozen corn. You're just going to fry all this, then add water, 1 cup at a time to make it your idea of soup.

Heat the butter and oil together first. I like to add the pepper then. Next comes the corn and garlic to sauté until soft. You can puree your tomatoes, or just skin and slice them. I suppose you might substitute with canned tomatoes; but if you're using canned corn as well, you might have just stayed depressed and made canned soup. People who can't afford to go to Indonesia eat a lot of that, after all. Seafood makes this a virtual dinner. Here's where I add shrimp. Then add water, 1 cup at a time while it simmers for an hour.

Baby,

Where Are you? I
Need your delicate smell.
I need the back of your
knees. I Also Need for you
to type some stuff for
Me. Soon, J.

Capon Soup for Handling Intractable People

Food

- Capon leftovers
- 2 bottles or cans beer
- 3 cups chopped red potatoes
- 1 cup chopped carrots
- 1 cup chopped celery with leaves and all
- Water

Action

Who wants to think about a castrated rooster boiled in its own juices? I do. Make Roast Capon with Tangerines Prepared in One Pan and Using One Knife (see Index) and eat most of it. It's already spiced to perfection, isn't it? Just remove any remaining stuffing, and place the entire creature in a big pot, like they do in cartoons, but cover it with the beer. Simmer this for an hour, or a couple of days, if you like. Skim the fat away all the while, because it's useless and vile, like some people who should be skimmed away from your life.

Now you can pour everything through a big colander into another pot, where the vegetables are waiting. Before you toss out the contents of the strainer, you can remove the capon pieces that have fallen away from the bone, and add them to your soup. Simmer all of this for an hour or so. You can add water to taste if you think it's getting too dense.

AMERICAN PSYCHOLOGY ASSOCIATION
Washington, DC

Dear Professor Angst,

Your request for funding for your proposed organization, "Cooks of Obsessive Compulsive Kitchens (COCK)" has been rejected. We are not required to produce any information about our decisions.

Thank you for your application.

Watercress Soup for Borderline Obsessive-Compulsives

Food

- 6 tablespoons butter
- 2 bunches watercress
- ½ cup milk and half-and-half combination, as in Potato Soup
- 1½ cups chicken stock
- Dash nutmeg
- Salt and black pepper to taste

Action

This is a perfect recipe for anyone with nervous energy because you have to stand around so much while you're making it; and because if you're not attending to details, you'll ruin it. Just let this boil once, and you've wrecked it.

Add rinsed watercress to the melted butter and cook about 5 minutes. That should give you enough time to alphabetize your spices. Put that through a blender or food processor for a couple of seconds, then bring it back to the pot with the milk mixture, stock, nutmeg, salt, and pepper, and heat it carefully for a bit until serving. You should have cleaned up the whole kitchen by now—except the pot you're using. You can garnish this soup with a bit of uncooked watercress.

Did the class meet your expectations based on the course
description? _see below_

Please use the space below for any additional comments
you may have regarding the course or the professor:

Professor Angst seems distraught
most times, and genuinely distracted.
I'm beginning to resent the constant
irrelevant references to food.

faculty evaluation form 38549

Roasted People Peppers

Food

- 2 yellow and 2 red peppers
- ½ cup olive oil

- Cayenne pepper to taste

Action

The best thing about preparing peppers is that you get to cut them into the shapes or initials of people who get on your nerves, douse them with red pepper, and more or less set them on fire. What could be better?

Remove the tops and seeds, as well as the hideous white stuff inside, and cut the peppers into letter forms or stick people. Then roast them under the broiler until the edges are black. Toss them about with oil and pepper, then arrange them on a plate.

Pseudo Moods Relaxation Centre
Center Yourself at the Centre

Dear Angst,

Let us then continue our unfortunate business on paper.

So you're saying that you asked for the silent flotation tank, but got a little Wagner piped in; and you're saying you DIDN'T want the light show. You still took the whole 40 minutes. You might have gotten dressed and come to the front desk.

While I am not willing to give you a refund or credit, if you come in for a SPA DAY SPECIAL, I will give you a Super Gandhi Calendar and floating stress ball.

Peace,

M.

Vicariously Marinated Eggplant

Food

- 2 large eggplants
- 1 teaspoon salt in enough water to cover the eggplants
- ½ cup red wine vinegar
- Black pepper to taste

- 1 clove garlic, crushed
- 1 teaspoon oregano
- 1 teaspoon basil
- Roasted peppers
- 1 cup olive oil

Action

This is a sort of quiet celebration of soaking things in other things. In the event that you might not get many opportunities to lounge about in gentle liquids, you can live it vicariously through your eggplants.

Cut the eggplants into cubes because slices will fall apart, and boil them for 5 minutes or so in the salted water. Make a dressing of vinegar, pepper, garlic, oregano, and basil, and toss this in a bowl with the roasted peppers. Let this rest in the refrigerator overnight, and add the oil just before serving.

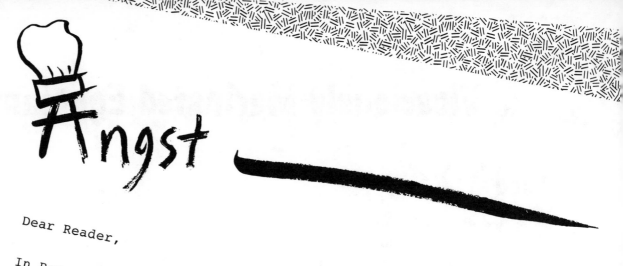

Angst

Dear Reader,

In Rome they say everything that goes in your mouth should be room temperature. (So how do they eat ice cream, which they do a lot?) It sure is true for salads. Nothing is more hideous than freezing lettuce served on a chilled plate. Cheap steak house style. Here is a salad that isn't slimy or cold and is beautiful to look upon.

Salad of Pears for the Easily Overstimulated

Food

- A few leaves soft lettuce plus a red leaf per serving
- 3 ripe pears, thinly sliced
- ⅔ cup chopped celery

- ¼ cup grated or slivered Romano
- Drizzle olive oil
- Black pepper to taste

Action

You're building this up on a plate rather like a small city. Start with laying out a bed of lettuce, then arrange sections of the pears in a formation that pleases you.

Sprinkle the celery on top, then the Romano over the whole creation. Next comes a soft rain of olive oil and pepper.

Dear Paul,

I wanted to apologize
for calling your new girlfriend Amelia
instead of Emily.
I really like Amelia,
and they rather look alike.
Even though you were only seeing her
for two weeks, I felt Amelia was one of us.

Your faithful friend who loves you dearly,

Angst

Salad of Red Cabbage to Quell Embarrassment

Food

- 1 average-sized head of red cabbage
- 1 small can white tuna packed in water
- ½ cup olive oil
- Black pepper to taste

Action

It's good to make red things when you're embarrassed, especially if you can chop them up vigorously, thereby undoing your own red-faced condition.

Chop up the cabbage finely until it's like shredded newspaper, and cut in the tuna with a fork. Toss this in a bowl with the oil and pepper. It's charming to serve this in little "bowls" that you can make of the rounder, tighter cabbage leaves as part of an antipasto tray. This tastes best after it's been setting a few hours.

Institute for Higher Self-Involvement
San Francisco - Gary - Telluride

Dear Professor Angst:

Thank you for agreeing to lecture on
"Spooky Sprouts: The Origins of Spell Casting and
Ground Vegetables"

A panel discussion including other accomplished food educators
will follow.

Although we charge a $250 fee* for each attendee, there is
unfortunately no compensation offered for your efforts. We
hope however, that this engagement will lead to other
invitations. Our guest list includes a number of cable television
producers and talk show hosts.

Yours in the self,
P. W.
Prairie Wonder

* Please make your check payable to the above, and be sure to
take advantage of our 10% speaker discount.

Salad of Broccoli and Carrots to Honor Their Mysteries

Food

- 6 or so young carrots, cut into thin strips
- 2 medium-sized stalks of broccoli
- ½ cup olive oil

- 1 clove garlic, crushed
- Salt and black pepper to taste
- Big handful pitted black olives
- Several basil leaves
- Dash ground coriander

Action

Carrots have been through a lot by the time you buy them, haven't they? They're locked away in the ground, throwing out roots, getting all connected with the earth, hearing all those stories, then just get ripped out. Oh well, might as well eat them.

I find it easier to slice carrots after they have been boiled for a short time, 2 minutes or so. You'll want to boil the broccoli too, then drain it, and cut it into small pieces. Toss all this with the oil, garlic, salt, and pepper. Then arrange the olives and basil leaves in there, and dust it lightly with coriander.

Sometimes I think I love you too much. Sometimes I think you love me too much. Yes, that's it, I'm feeling kind of smothered. I'm not exactly sure if I want a relationship now.

J.

Blue Cheese and Tomatoes for Ambiguous Relationships

Food

- 2 fabulous tomatoes
- ¼ cup olive oil
- ¼ cup balsamic vinegar

- ½ pound crumbly blue cheese
- Black pepper to taste
- 4 basil leaves

Action

So many people have a problem with blue cheese: they didn't like it as children, it smells strongly, it aggravates allergies—whatever. It's good to serve it to someone you're not sure of because there's that high likelihood that they'll absolutely hate it and not be able to tell you.

This is as simple as it seems: the toma-toes are an excuse to eat the cheese, the cheese is an excuse to eat the tomatoes. Slice the tomatoes and arrange them on a plate. Pour the oil and vinegar over them, then crumble the cheese on top; season with pepper. Basil leaves make a beautiful garnish.

Angst

Dear Reader,

When I was a kid living in New Orleans, my teacher
told me that olives are the most potent of the
enchanted foods.
She said if you whispered your troubles into the core
of an olive, then cooked it, the trouble would dissolve
away.

Here's a way to cook out a whole world of troubles.

Salad of Green Olives That Can Be Trusted with Your Secrets

Food

- 1 average-sized jar pitted green olives
- 1 cup chopped celery
- 1 red onion, minced
- ½ cup balsamic vinegar
- Cayenne pepper to taste
- ½ cup olive oil

Action

OK, so you can't cook the olives here. I still think they'd be interested in hearing about your problems. Soaking them in vinegar could do well to burn your troubles away in a pool of acid, though.

Toss the olives, celery, and onion together with the vinegar and pepper and refrigerate overnight. Add the oil just before serving.

AMERICAN PSYCHOLOGY ASSOCIATION
Washington, DC

Dear Professor Angst,

Your proposal for funding for a symposium on "Kitchens of the Inner Child" has been rejected. The materials you propose to use are too difficult to obtain. Requiring lifetime dream journals from every applicant to a cooking program is objectively unreasonable. And your demand for the 3000 word essay, "How Cooking Saved Me from Having to Grow Up" is a violation of your students' privacy.

You might review our mission statement before you apply again.

Salad of Lettuce and Starfruit to Amuse Your Inner Child

Food

- Several leaves romaine, torn into pieces
- 1 head radicchio, cut into strips
- Balsamic vinegar
- 1 beautiful starfruit

Action

Buying starfruit is like buying toys. It feels so special and frivolous. You might make an announcement to your inner child, like, "I'm buying this starfruit just for you because I think you're so, so special." And then your inner child will say to your unconscious, "But I want Pez."

Make a bed of the lettuces and cover it with a light film of vinegar. Arrange the starfruit atop and look at it for a while before you eat it.

Dear Angst,

I (can) cannot (circle one) attend your
"Watch Every Episode of 60 Minutes From 1977-81 In A
Row" Party.

Kisses:

Paul
_____
Your name here

P.S.
I'm Bringing Amelia

Celebratory Celery Heart Salad

Food

- 2 Macintosh apples, peeled, cored, and chopped
- ½ cup cream
- Large pile of chopped celery hearts
- ½ cup olive oil
- ½ cup lemon juice

Action

Heat the apples in the cream gently for a few minutes while you toss together the other items. When the apples and cream have cooled, toss them into the rest of the salad. Serve this to your guests, unless they are so stimulated and entertained by other things that one more event might be too much.

MAINSTREAM MUSIC

Topeka, Kansas

Dear Professor Angst:

Your lyrics for <u>Is This God, Or Only Meatloaf</u> were intriguing, but not quite right for Mainstream.

You might try one of the Christian Rock houses.

Good luck.

Elvis Davis
President

Supernatural Meatloaf

Food

- ½ cup bread crumbs made from dried crusts of Italian bread
- ½ cup Parmesan
- Rosemary and sage to taste
- 1 clove garlic, crushed
- 2 pounds ground sirloin

- 1 pound ground pork
- 2 tablespoons flour
- 4 tablespoons butter
- 1½ cups red wine
- 1½ cups water
- Sliced carrots
- Chopped celery

Action

People who bake their meatloaf will seem to you like misguided fools after you've tasted this. You won't even want to call it meatloaf, with all those common connotations.

Work smashed bread crumbs, Parmesan, spices, and garlic into the combined meats until you have formed a loaf. Dust the whole thing generously with flour. Then, in a pot on top of the stove, brown the floured meat in the butter on all sides, about 10 minutes each. Then add alternate cups of wine and water every 10 minutes until an hour has passed. In the last half hour, you can drop in vegetables. The gravy is from heaven.

Dear Professor Angst,

Thanks for teaching me that new exercice that stops those annoying voices in my head. I got rid of everyone but Anais Nin—blah, blah blah all day long.

I also wanted to thank you for letting me use your name as a reference for this job I'm trying to get in the bakery at Mucha Mocha. I guess I should have asked you before I put in the application.

Oh well, here I am asking you now.

Thanx.

Your special student,
Charlotte

A Cleansing Ritual of Lemon Steaks

Food

- 2 lemons
- ½ cup olive oil
- ½ cup butter, melted

- Salt and black pepper to taste
- 2 porterhouse steaks

Action

Here's something to make when you want to purify your life of noise and irritation. Squeeze the juice of one of the lemons and make a dressing of the juice, oil, melted butter, salt, and pepper. Slice the other lemon and arrange the slices in a bowl large enough for the steaks to lay flat. You want to sandwich the steaks between lemon slices. Then pour your dressing over the whole thing and refrigerate overnight.

The next day, discard the lemon slices and broil the steaks to your liking in the marinade. Whatever was annoying you when you started slicing lemons 24 hours ago will seem like old news now.

Did the class meet your expectations based on the course

description?

Please use the space below for any additional comments
you may have regarding the course or the professor:

NICE LUNGS   PROF ANGST!!!

Pepper Steaks with Pain

Food

- 4 tablespoons whole peppercorns
- 4 filet mignon steaks
- 4 tablespoons butter, melted
- 4 tablespoons oil
- 4 tablespoons cognac
- 1 cup half-and-half

Action

Wrap the peppercorns in a clean towel, lay it on the floor, and jump on it mercilessly for as long as you can. Think of the towel of peppercorns as a roomful of ingrates, poor listeners, and wanton failures. Rub the crushed pepper into the steaks and fry them in the melted butter and oil, turning them once. When they're nearly done to your liking, douse them with cognac and set them afire. They deserve it. Remove the steaks from the pan and quickly pour the cream into the pan juices. Maintain a low heat while you stir this up for a beautiful sauce.

Mega Maids Inc.

"We'll Clean Anything..."

Dear Angst,

You place undue stress on our slogan, "We'll clean anything." Your kitchen simply cannot be contended with by only one team of highly trained professionals.

Should you require our services in the future, please be prepared to be billed at two times our regular rate. Sorry.

...Unless This Letter Indicates Otherwise"

Roast Capon with Tangerines Prepared in One Pan and Using One Knife

Food

- 4- to 6-pound capon, washed and creepy stuff inside removed
- 3 tangerines, peeled
- ½ cup butter

- Herb mixture of fennel seed, oregano, parsley, rosemary, and thyme to make about ½ cup
- Salt and white pepper to taste

Action

Line a roasting pan with aluminum foil so that you have disposable postcapon grunge. Place whole tangerines in the birds. Don't squeeze them or rub juice into the bird—it's overstimulating. Rub butter and herbs into the skin, then salt and pepper. Cover with a tent of foil for the first 45 minutes of baking at 375 degrees, then remove the foil and broil for 10 to 15 minutes.

It is the year One.
You are ruler of the Year.
Your lips rule all
That is spoken in the
Year One.

Raven

New Orleans—Style Lamb Chops

Food

- ¼ cup Dijon mustard
- 2 or 3 loin or rib lamb chops per person
- ¼ cup butter
- Salt and black pepper to taste
- ½ cup white wine with a splash of balsamic vinegar added

Action

Don't make this for just anybody. It's too powerful—you'll see. You take these relatively ordinary ingredients and come out with something from another world.

Spread the mustard on the meat, then apply bits of butter all over, then salt and pepper. Broil on each side to your liking. Arrange the lamb chops on a plate and add the vinegar-wine combination to the hot juices in the pan. Warm them together for 5 minutes or so, and use as a sauce for the meat.

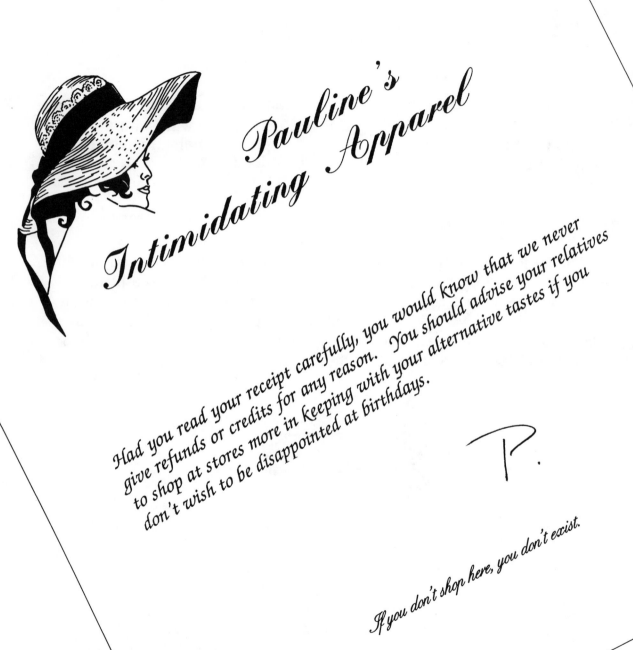

Pauline's Intimidating Apparel

Had you read your receipt carefully, you would know that we never give refunds or credits for any reason. You should advise your relatives to shop at stores more in keeping with your alternative tastes if you don't wish to be disappointed at birthdays.

P.

If you don't shop here, you don't exist.

Garlic Pork for Overcoming Pigheaded Types

Food

- 4 butterfly pork chops
- 4 cloves garlic, cut into slivers
- Rosemary leaves
- Cloves
- Small amount olive oil
- 2 cups chianti or other red wine
- Salt and black pepper to taste

Action

Jab the pork with a knife repeatedly as hard as you can. Now you've made little folds into which you insert the garlic slivers, rosemary leaves, and cloves. Coat the meat with a film of olive oil and bake in a pool of red wine for 40 minutes at 400 degrees. Sprinkle with salt and pepper.

AMERICAN PSYCHOLOGY ASSOCIATION
Washington, DC

Dear Professor Angst,

Your grant application for a 12-Step approach for salad making has been rejected by our board.

We suggest you review our mission statement before you exert yourself any further.

12-Step Steak Salad

Food

- Steak leftovers from some other magnificent feast
- Romaine leaves
- Arugula lettuce
- Small red onion
- 1 tomato
- Balsamic vinegar for sprinkling
- Olive oil for drizzling
- Salt and black pepper to taste

Action

1. Acknowledge your need for a perfect salad to come home to.
2. Thank yourself for saving the leftovers.
3. Slice steak into thin strips.
4. Arrange a bed of romaine.
5. Prepare a coverlet of arugula.
6. Mince onion.
7. Slice tomato.
8. Toss onion, tomato, and steak together.
9. Sprinkle that vinegar, drizzle that oil, and shake that salt and pepper onto the meat mixture.
10. Transfer this to your bed of lettuces.
11. Eat it.
12. Offer thanks to the great power that gave you cows to eat.

It has come to my aTTeNtiOn that you are

Hitting On RaVen, my natural love.

Want to die? Get oUt of hiS faCe.

DOn't sEE him agAin.

DON't lOok at him.

Trout Hate Mail

Food

- 1 cleaned and prepared trout
- 4 tablespoons butter
- Juice of one lemon

- 1 teaspoon parsley
- ½ cup white wine
- Salt and white pepper to taste

Action

Make an envelope of brown paper, even a clean grocery bag, and lay in the fish. Examine the logistics of mailing this to someone just the way it is right now. Melt the butter in a little saucepan with everything else, then pour into the envelope. Bake on a flat rack at 400 degrees for 20 minutes.

from video club Mall

VIDEO IDIOTS

Dear Angst,

You have repeatedly ignored our requests that you return **Whore**, now ten weeks overdue. Will no amount of threats or begging affect you? You might like to know that this tape has been requested by an elderly gentleman who struggles in daily hoping that you have finally returned it. Please drop it off at your nearest convenience.

DON'T FORGET ABOUT OUR TWO
FOR ONE WEDNESDAY!!!

BE SURE TO COME BY!!!

THE MANAGEMENT

The Forgetful Person's Marinated Tuna

Food

- 1 pound tuna steak
- ½ cup olive oil
- Juice of one lemon

- 1 clove garlic, crushed
- Crushed fennel seeds
- Salt and white pepper to taste

Action

Set tuna in a baking dish while you combine all the ingredients for the marinade. Pour the mixture over the tuna and keep it refrigerated for 3 or 4 hours. Don't forget it's there. Bake for 20 minutes at 350 degrees, then broil it for 5 minutes to brown the top.

NOTICE OF FINAL DETERMINATION
BUREAU OF PARKING
312-555 BOOT

To The Registered Owner or Lessee Of: **IL   ANGST**

Ms. Angst

VIOLATION NOTICE NO.	DATE AND TIME OF VIOLATION	LOCATION	VIOLATION CODE/ DESCRIPTION	FINE AMOUNT	PENALTY AMOUNT	TOTAL
0006665707	09-10 1002 A	1925 BURLING OTHR 12-31	0964040B STREET CLEANING	$25.00	$25.00	$50.00

Thanks for the car. Sorry about this, but they never come after you. You need oil. I'm dying for you. Bye J.

Roast Chicken with Olives Parked Inside

Food

- 1 small white onion, finely chopped
- ½ cup butter, melted
- 1 regular-sized jar pitted green olives
- 1 cup cranberries

- 1 cup chopped celery
- 2 cups bread crumbs softened in white wine
- Large roasting chicken
- Salt and white pepper to taste

Action

Think of the chicken as your car, and the olives as every undeserved ticket you have ever got. You may need to buy several birds. Sauté the onion in the butter until browned and add to a tossed mixture of all the other items as they are. Stuff the chicken with these wonderful things. You can baste this with more melted butter, and add salt and pepper while the bird is roasting at 375 degrees for an hour or so.

KnoW any blAck magic?

I do...

I've got the candles to Wreck

yOur Life LOser

De-Hexing Marinated Pork

Food

- ½ cup chianti or other red wine
- ½ cup balsamic vinegar
- 1 clove garlic, crushed
- 1 bay leaf

- 1 tablespoon each: thyme, juniper berries, minced scallion
- Salt and black pepper to taste
- 4 pork chops

Action

Place everything but the pork chops in a saucepan and gently boil for a couple of minutes. When it cools, pour it over the pork chops and refrigerate overnight. You are now soaking a pig in boiled acid—a small comfort. Later melt some butter and fry the pork chops for 10 minutes on each side before pouring in the marinade. Then cook another 20 minutes.

OFFICIAL ENTRY FORM
THE YOUNG REPUBLICANS SCHOLARSHIP COMMITTEE

Attach your essay entitled:

"The Worst Job I Ever Had and How It Improved My Life"

Name: Megan

Current Position: Asst. Chef/Combatant of lost hope

Job you intend to describe: Removing the intestines, hearts and livers of frozen chickens as they drop from a convey or belt

What qualifies you for this scholarship? I have continued to love and defend chickens everywhere

Address:

City:

Work Phone

Home Phone

PROFESSOR Angst,

Would you please critique my scholarship application

Thanx Megan ☺

Warm, Friendly Chicken Breasts in Marsala

Food

- ½ cup olive oil
- ½ cup butter
- Small pile of flour
- Salt and white pepper to taste

- 2 boned and skinned chicken breasts
- 1 cup Marsala

Action

Melt the oil and butter together, then add in flour, salt, and pepper. Fry your chicken breasts gently and tenderly on each side until you're convinced they're done. Don't speak harshly to anyone nearby during this process. After cooking, remove the chicken and pour Marsala in the hot pan, and cook it down to a sauce. Pour that creation over the awaiting chicken.

My dear unique and wonderful _angst_,

I can't believe myself. After pails full of passionate tears, hours of toil and anxious days of waiting, I have finally been awarded a grant to open a cooking school in Milan!

Of course, I'll have to take a crash course in cooking somewhere so I can really be qualified. I also feel, and this is a true feeling, that if I just open the school and let the Milanese express themselves from deep down within - then good meals are certain to follow. Of course, I'm writing mostly to invite all of you to join me this summer. The fees are super reasonable.

Bon Apetito!

agnés

(Say AHN-YAY)

Soft Eggs for When You're Feeling Manipulated

Food

- 2 eggs
- 2 tablespoons butter
- Parsley
- Chives
- Lemon juice
- Salt and black pepper to taste

Action

Boil your eggs for 4 minutes, no more. Immediately run them under cold water and shell them. Slice them down the middle and arrange on a plate. Make a sauce of the remaining ingredients by heating them gently over a low flame, then pour it over the eggs. This must be eaten immediately—so don't wait around.

HAIR FOR DAYS

CALL 1-900-555-HAIR

Dear Ms. Angst:

We're awfully sorry about your recent haircut. I thought you were exaggerating on the telephone; but when I saw you, I was stunned. You look terrible! I can see what you mean - it will take years for that to grow out.

Our problem here is that we can't identify the person who 'did' you. I don't think anyone of that description has ever worked here. Certainly no one with that name.

We'll do our best to make this up to you. It's not like we can just offer you a new haircut though - I mean, there's nothing to cut. Sorry.

Yours,

The Management

Prosciutto Eggs That May Not Look So Great, But Are Really Wonderful Inside

Food

- 6 eggs, hard-boiled, peeled, and sliced down the center
- 3 slices prosciutto, minced
- 5 or 6 tiny dill pickles

- 2 tablespoons mayonnaise
- Shake dry mustard
- Black pepper to taste
- Watercress leaves for garnish

Action

Remove the egg yolks and smooth them out with a fork until they stop looking like bald heads. Add in everything else except the watercress and mix it through. Fill the egg whites with the paste and garnish with a couple of watercress leaves.

Dear Professor Angst,

We are currently forming an on-campus organization, MAD (Mothers Against Dads), to accommodate
the single mothers here. SInce the Academy
currently funds the club DAM (Dads Against Mothers), we feel
we are morethan deserving.

Our immediate requirements include: a private meeting center,
which we would like to refer to as the MAD Temple, a
full time administrator and an on-site caterer for every
meeting. Since we have yet to acquire these things, we hoped
to appeal to your generous spirit in asking
that you provide the food for our charter meeting.

How About it, Professor?

We are expecting somewhere between 10 and 1,000
people.

Naomee

Andrea

Cyndi

ayn

Heartless Cucumber Sandwiches

Food

- 2 cucumbers, peeled and sliced as thinly as possible
- Balsamic vinegar
- 1 teaspoon oregano
- Oatmeal bread slices, crust removed

- Mayonnaise
- Several thin slices of Swiss cheese
- Handful watercress

Action

Soak the cucumber slices in vinegar and oregano for an hour or so, then drain them on paper. Your sandwiches should be built like this: bread, mayonnaise, cheese, cucumbers, watercress, bread (no mayonnaise against the watercress side). For some reason, people think these are the best sandwiches in the world, but they take nothing to prepare. So you get credit for making a big effort, even if your heart isn't in it.

Love your New Look.
Did they Find THat meAn girl Who did it?

Pita Pizza for When You're Inclined to Cut Things

Food

- ¼ cup olive oil
- 1 tomato, sliced
- 6 mushrooms, sliced
- Small amounts minced white onion and green pepper

- 1 clove garlic, crushed
- Dash oregano
- 1 round pita bread
- 1 egg

Action

You just need one knife to take care of this project, so make this when you feel especially like using a knife. Toss together olive oil and vegetables with the garlic and oregano, and lay them atop your pita bed. Break an egg over the top and place in a 400-degree oven. You'll want to eat this when the egg is visibly cooked.

Hi Hon,

I can't believe how really juicy psychology is. Who would have thought I could get into grad school for social work with my theatre major? I'm counting the days until I can sit across my sprawling white sofa and get paid for listening to all that dirt.

Way to go me.

Justine

P. S.   All the men here have cute beards!

French Toast for Amateurs

Food

- 3 large eggs
- Small piles allspice, cinnamon, and salt
- 2 tablespoons butter
- 2 tablespoons oil
- Several slices white bread without the crust
- Confectioners' sugar

Action

Whisk the eggs and pile in the spices and salt while you're melting the butter and oil together in a frying pan. Soak the bread slices, a minute at a time, in the egg mixture, then fry them quickly on both sides. You can shake a bit of confectioners' sugar over the toast before serving.

DREAM JOURNAL

My grandmother finally gives me the Fiesta Ware she's got packed away in her cabin on Cayuga Lake. I can't believe my good fortune. I uncover the plates slowly, wash them, arrange them, read the old newspapers they were wrapped in. Over the radio comes a warning - anyone possessing Fiesta Ware should be advised that they contain harmful levels of toxic paint. People holding Fiesta Ware will be fined $5000 per plate, $2500 per bowl and cups are $1000 each. Fortunately, the moon turns blood red, the sky fills with black feathers, the apocalypse commences, and I don't have to pay.

Caviar Sandwiches Made in Heaven

Food

- The prettiest crackers you can buy, especially if they're made with rye
- Minced red onions
- Bit of cream cheese
- Red caviar
- Tiny sprigs parsley

Action

You could hum while you put this together. Mince the onions so they are really tiny. Spread cream cheese on the crackers, then comes the onion, with a nest of caviar on top. Then come the tiniest bits of parsley spread atop of that. This is especially good with a strong cup of coffee.

Toasted Cheese Sandwich, All in One Color for People Who Spill Things

Food

- 2 slices white bread
- 1 egg
- Small square of cream cheese
- Some grated Gruyère
- Salt and white pepper to taste

Action

First toast the bread, then combine everything else in a saucepan. Heat it slowly and quietly until it becomes smooth and heavy. Spread it over the toast, then broil the whole creation for a minute or two. If you drop it in your lap while you're eating it, it should just rub in nicely, except for the toast, which you can gently extract.

∉ngst

Dear Charlotte,

You must have been terribly upset to call me last night at 3:00 AM. I'm sure I wasn't very helpful- I'm not so lucid at that hour; and I certainly shouldn't be your first choice for romantic advice.

Here's a model that seems to work: Think of people as falling into one of three types, more like Daffy Duck, more like Bugs Bunny, or more like Elmer Fudd. If you can stand the alienation and uncaring sarcasm, Daffy Duck types are the most fun. If you crave security, warmth and spontaneous friendliness, you'll like Bugs Bunny types. They always come out on top. Elmer Fudd types are to be avoided, unless your urge to nurture others is so profound that you are blinded to all other qualifications. There you have everything I know about romantic relationships. I hope it helps.

Yours sincerely,

A.

Professor Angst

Late Night Pasta Sauce

Food

- 4 tomatoes, peeled and seeded
- 1 clove garlic, crushed
- 6 tablespoons olive oil
- Medium-sized pile basil and mint leaves

Action

Just cook these things, that's all. You could get really sleepy, just keep the heat low and there shouldn't be any problems.

There's a refreshing mint event taking place here to get you ready for the shock of toothpaste in the morning.

THE ACADEMY FOR WEALTHY SOCIALISTS

Dear Professor Angst:

We regret that we must deny your request for subscriptions to:

Journal of Shopping and Food Deprivation
Cooking Rules for the Unruly
Food and Mood

As you should know, we require six copies of the form, "Rationale for Periodical Order," which should be accompanied by a 1,000-word description for your intended use of the publications.

Yours sincerely,

The Dean's Committee on Magazine Appropriation

Dinner for Two for Two Bucks

Food

- 4 red potatoes
- Extra-virgin olive oil
- Small pile fennel seed
- Small pile ground coriander

- 1 clove garlic, crushed
- Red leaf lettuce
- Lemon juice

Action

Slice the potatoes as thinly as possible. Try not to think of your ancestors doing the same thing on a boat. Avoid flashbacks of the Disney cartoon version of *Jack and the Beanstalk* where Mickey slices up a lentil bean as if it were a meatloaf and serves it to his impoverished family. You need a saucepan with a circumference somewhere between the size of a 45 and an LP. Pour in an inch of extra-virgin olive oil. Heat it slowly, but let it get ridiculously hot before you throw in the spices and potatoes. You could do all this in a frying pan, but the angry flecks of hot oil may annoy your wrists, and the splattering of oil about the kitchen creates a white-trash effect. You can add the garlic now. Fry and turn the slices until clearly done, then drain them on elegant wedding invitations. Make your salad of lettuce only with a drizzle of oil and lemon juice. Dine in the vindicated glory of simple pleasure.

SEIZURE NOTICE
BUREAU OF PARKING
312-555-BOOT

To The Registered Owner or Lessee Of: IL   ANGST

Ms. Angst

VIOLATION NOTICE NO.	DATE AND TIME OF VIOLATION	LOCATION	VIOLATION CODE/ DESCRIPTION	FINE AMOUNT	PENALTY AMOUNT	TOTAL

Hummus with Garnish to Conquer Ennui

Food

- 1 can garbanzo beans
- 1 clove garlic
- Juice of half a lemon
- Tahini as needed

- Sumac powder
- Parsley
- Black olives

Action

Drain the garbanzo beans, but save some of that liquid in case you need it for thinning. Place in a food processor the beans, garlic, lemon juice, and slowly add tahini to thicken. Whip this into a smooth paste, adding more tahini or liquid as needed.

Spread this on a plate. Looks pathetic, doesn't it? Sort of like an empty parking space. If you're not too depressed, decorate it with the sumac powder, parsley, and olives, then park in triangles of warmed pita.

HIRSCH'S CLEANERS

We did the Pope!

Dear Angst,

Lost some blood-stained old lady suit you brought in.
Sorry.

Can't find it.
Sorry.

H.

Stain-Wielding Tomatoes and Carrots in Coriander

Food

- 1 medium-sized white onion
- 4 tablespoons butter
- Salt and cayenne pepper to taste
- 1 tomato, skinned, seeds removed, and minced
- 8 or 10 carrots, sliced into thin strips
- Small pile ground coriander

Action

Put on something red or orange, and be sure it's washable. Chop the onion and brown in melted butter in a large frying pan. Add salt and cayenne pepper. Next add tomato and let that cook a few minutes. Now pile in the carrots and pour on enough water to barely cover them. This should create a tremendous splashing effect. Cook all this over medium heat for 20 minutes or so. Just before serving, toss the vegetables with the coriander until they are coated throughout.

6. Why are they called spare ribs?

7. How did the Magicians of the 6th Century use asparagus?

8. Why are raspberries so tiny in the winter?

9. (BONUS) What is it all about, anyway? What is this thing called life?

Vegetable Motley Crew

Food

- ½ cup olive oil
- Juice of one lemon
- 1 clove garlic, crushed
- Tiny pile cinnamon
- 1 eggplant

- 1 yellow pepper
- 5 or 6 asparagus stalks
- 1 tomato
- Black olives
- Parsley

Action

Make a dressing of the first four ingredients. Prepare the vegetables by roasting them on a flat pan under a broiler for 5 minutes. First cube the eggplant, cut the pepper into strips, cut the asparagus into 1-inch sections, and cut the tomato into wedges after removing the seeds. Toss the vegetables in a bowl with the dressing, and add olives and chopped parsley to make it really beautiful.

Did the class meet your expectations based on the course
description?_____
_____
_____
_____

Please use the space below for any additional comments
you may have regarding the course or the professor:

WHILE I'M inSpiReD BY THE PROFESSOR'S inTENSE MONOLOGUES.
THEY lack A REAL WORLD quality. AND AS A RESULT, THE
STUDENT is lEFT FLOATING ADRIFT iN A MEANINGLESS
SEA OF RHETORIC. SHE'S NOT VERY PUNCTUAL EITHER.
AND I think IF SHE'S GONNA BRING BREAKFAST
SHE SHOULD BRING ENOUGH FOR THE WHOLE CLASS.

faculty evaluation form 38549

Eggplant Cakes to Eat All Day

Food

- 1 large eggplant
- 1 egg
- 1 teaspoon baking powder
- 1 cup sugar

- Salt to taste
- Enough oil to cover your frying pan

Action

Peel the eggplant and boil for 7 or 8 minutes, then mash it like potatoes. Add everything else to the eggplant; and thicken it with a little flour if you need to. You want a spackle-like consistency. (In fact, you could probably use this as a spackle, but it wouldn't store very well.) Form little cakes of this "batter" and fry them on both sides until brown. Sprinkle them with sugar if it's early in the day, with salt if it's late.

MESSAGE FROM MEGAN

Dear Prof Angst,

Sorry I spilled coffee on all the mid terms.
Sorry I didn't get to any of the work you left for me.
I had to leave early again because my grandmother died.
Not my grandmother who died last week, and not the one
who died three weeks ago. This woman, well, she wasn't
my blood relative, but she was more like a grandma than
the others. I may not have ever mentioned her, but we
were really, really close. Sorry.

Thanx Megan
☺

Cold Vegetables in Hazelnut Oil for Accident-Prone Types

Food

- ½ cup each hazelnut oil and kiwi vinegar
- Dill
- Salt and black pepper to taste
- 1 zucchini
- Handful peapods
- Quartered mushrooms

Action

This is a good recipe for accident-prone types, because so little actual cooking takes place. Make a dressing of the oil and vinegar, dill, salt, and pepper. Boil the zucchini and peapods for just seconds, then let them cool. The mushrooms needn't be cooked. Slice the zucchini into slivers. Then toss everything together and refrigerate a while before serving.

R—I want to punch you right here. ↙

—Angst

Jalapeño Corn Bread to Surprise an Unwitting Opponent

Food

- 1 package cheapest possible corn bread mix
- Picante sauce
- 1 more egg than the mix requires

Action

You can make your own corn bread out of boxed cornmeal, but if you're using something from a box, you didn't really make it anyway. Why not just go all the way and use a mix? They all are great, if you ask me. You simply substitute picante sauce where it calls for milk, and thin it out with an extra egg. This is one of those recipes that will make you seem deceptively accomplished for no reason.

DREAM JOURNAL

Last night I dreamt that a traveling band of magicians worked my kitchen over, Cinderella style, so that everything was hyper brand new, untouched and perfect. All appliances were manufactured by the same company at the same time, and the original boxes were stored neatly in cabinets that were designed just for that. All the rebate cards had been filled out and mailed in for me.

I opened the utensil drawer marked (in magnificent type) A-H to a gleaming world of accomplishments in the kitchen design universe. Unfortunately, I didn't feel like cooking in that dream. I just felt like standing around.

Very Inactive Peapods in Sugar

Food

- 2 tablespoons each olive oil and unsweetened butter
- Enough peapods to line your frying pan, washed
- Even sprinkle of sugar to cover

Action

Very little movement and virtually no utensils are required here. Just melt the oil and butter together before placing the peapods in the pan. Sprinkle them with sugar while they're getting cooked through, but not limp. The peapods, that is. You just watch.

Dear Angst,

I saw you notice me at the recent opening for
Garth Vap's photographs of anguished monkeys. I
was wearing the orange poncho, and was smiling.
I just wanted to say that you look like the kind
of woman who could really help me out a lot, and
if you want to go out or something, you could
come to Mucha Mocha where I work.
Here's my schedule:
Sunday: 7-4, then gone from 4 until 4:15, then
           4:15-8
Monday: 11-2, then 3:15-7
Tuesday: I'm at the studio all day.
Wednesday: 7-10, then 11-8
Thursday: 8-10, then 12-4:15
Friday: I'm not sure what I do on Fridays or
           Saturdays.

Really hoping something comes of this.

                    Helmut

Raspberry Ice for Time Worshippers

Food

- Equal amounts of water, sugar, raspberries, and lemon juice

Action

People who are obsessed with the time should go for this. There is very little cooking but much clock watching. Heat the water and sugar together until thick, then cool it off. Add strained raspberries and lemon juice, and put the whole thing into a wide bowl. Freeze it for 25-minute periods, removing it at the end of each session to smash it up a bit, then refreeze it over and over until it looks like Italian ice.

The fact that I did not return your gift of pears in chocolate is not necessarily an indication that I would have time to speak to you if you called.

Enclosed please find some literature I've saved from a workshop on heightening your sensitivity.

Carole

Pears in Chocolate for Begging Forgiveness

Food

- 2 beautiful pears
- Bit of water as needed
- 2 squares unsweetened chocolate

- 4 tablespoons sugar
- Whipped cream

Action

Slice the pears thinly and set them in a pan with a light cover of water. Gently poach them for 5 minutes. Remove them from the pan and arrange them in a baking dish, but leave the liquid in the pan. Bring in the chocolate now, and melt that in the pear liquid until smooth and blended. Add the sugar last, blend it all together, then pour it over the awaiting pears. Bake all this loveliness at 300 degrees for 10 minutes or so, and serve with a garnish of whipped cream if you like.

Dear Angst,

I am unable to attend your "COME AS YOU WERE" party this weekend. You seem to be mocking the idea of past lives by suggesting we dress up as someone we used to be.

Angst, I don't find one thing humorous about my past lives. They were a tremendous burden to me - trying to rule an entire nation, launching several revolutions, being mercilessly slaughtered for my tusks - I earned my way to this charmed station with faith and endurance.

Yes, you have hurt my feelings.

I suppose while you and your friends who smoke are carrying on, making fun of those of us who invented this universe, I'll be meditating on my own special gifts.

Your special friend, nonetheless,

agnés

(Say AHN-YAY)

Pears with Allspice for Time Travel

Food

- 2 beautiful pears
- Small pile allspice and sugar combined

- 1 square of vanilla ice cream

Action

Here is a recipe that you could have made during any one of your post–11th-century lives, assuming you lived in an arctic region where vanilla and allspice were accessible. Slice the pears thinly and toss them in the allspice and sugar until all pieces are coated well. Lay them on a baking dish and warm them in a 300-degree oven for 5 minutes. Transfer them to a little sofa of vanilla ice cream and serve immediately.

Angst,

Here's what I learned this week. It's so cool. The whole human experience thing is basically stacked in layers that go like this:

Spiritual - that's the highest - it's the soul, and it's a girl layer.

Intellectual - next highest - it's the mind, a male layer (right!)

Emotional - the heart, that's a girl thing.

Physical - the lowest, a totally guy layer to be sure. You see, Angst, everyone has all these parts. Some of them are masculine and some of them are feminine and you can be one and still sort of be in the other. Grad school is so meaningful!

Justine

Total Human Experience Apples

Food

- 4 Macintosh apples
- ½ cup white wine
- ½ cup sugar
- Bit vanilla extract
- 4 egg whites

Action

Peel and slice the apples nicely and cook them in a pan with the wine, sugar, and vanilla. Drain them on paper towels, then make a bed of them in a baking dish. Beat the egg whites into a meringue and cover the apples. Then bake the whole thing at 300 degrees for 15 minutes. Notice how the apples represent the earth—the physical world; sugar creates emotions; wine is intellectual, because you speak so intelligently when you've been drinking it; and the white cloud atop this is, of course, the spiritual world.

Pauline's
Intimidating Apparel

Angst,

Aren't you cute?
Yes, we'll be happy to meet you in small claims court.
I certainly hope for your sake that you have as many prominent
attorneys in your family as I do.

P.

If you don't shop here, you don't exist.

Ladyfingers

Food

- 6 eggs, separated
- 1 cup sugar
- Salt

- 2 cups flour
- Tiny bit confectioners' sugar

Action

You are making two batters, one of yolks and one of whites, then combining them. Beat the yolks and most of the sugar together with a dash of salt. Cut the flour in slowly. Now beat the egg whites into a froth, cutting in a bit of the remaining sugar. Then combine the two batters. The best way to distribute the batter onto the baking sheet is through a pastry tube, where you just squeeze "fingers" onto the sheet. Dust the dough with confectioners' sugar and again after baking at 375 degrees for 10 minutes.

Dear Angst,

I'm beginning to have second thoughts about my new career in the helping profession. Today they assigned us our fieldwork placements.

All I can say is GROSS!

I like the idea of cocaine babies as much as anyone. But I didn't know we were going to have to hold them and stuff.

Call me or something.

Justine

Rude-Awakening Nectarine Pudding

Food

- 6 very ripe nectarines
- ½ cup butter
- ½ cup sugar
- Small pile allspice
- Arrowroot or ginger cookies

Action

Peel the nectarines and cut them into pieces. They don't have to look nice at all, because you're going to mash them anyway. Cook them in melted butter a few minutes, then pile in sugar and spice and cook another few minutes. You can process this in a machine, but it's just as easy to mash this mixture in a bowl until you find smoothness. It looks so much like baby food now, you'll wonder why you didn't just buy a jar of baby peaches instead. But then you'll taste it. Spread this sweetly over little cookies.

Dear Angst,

I realized my schedule was a little different last week. I figure you got my letter on Tuesday, and had you come in on Wednesday between 11 and 12:30. I wouldn't have been there. I was at this new class I'm taking in developing my awareness of world strife. Attached is my work schedule for this week. Also, you can always stop by my studio. I don't have a doorbell, so throw your keys up at the third floor window in back where the trucks are parked. Anytime is OK. I'm never doing anything.

Really hoping something comes of this.

Helmut

Co-Dependent Coffee Ice

Food

- 1 cup remarkable coffee with sugar, even if you don't take sugar in coffee you drink

- 1 cup water

Action

Pour everything into the glass pitcher that belongs to your drip coffeemaker and turn on the warming plate. Let it sit there for a little while, but don't let it burn. Otherwise, cook the above on top of a double boiler for 10 minutes, and let it cool. Pour it all into a bowl that can tolerate the freezer. Take it out and rough it up every 20 minutes or so, the way you would for Raspberry Ice. (See Index.)

```
        LIP'S WINE BAR &
           TRATTORIA

                          5:47PM
CHECK     7
JOSELYN  GUESTS  2

JOSELYN
   BEVERAGE          1.00
   COFFEE            5.50
   CALAMARI FRT
   VERMICELLI       11.95
   ALFREDO           1.95
   ADD VEG
   CONGHILIE        10.95
   MARINARA          2.95
   ADD CHICKEN
   CAPPUCCINO        2.50
   CAPPUCCINO

                     36.80
SUBTOT                3.04
TAX                  39.84
TOTAL

HAPPY HOUR 4-7 SEVEN NIGHTS A WEEK
OPEN FOR DINNER SEVEN NIGHTS A WEEK
28 DRAFT BEERS, 50 WINES BY THE GLASS
```

Evidence of the best night ever.

Strawberries for Valentine's Day

Food

- 2 pints of beautiful strawberries, leaves removed and sliced in halves like little unbroken hearts

- ½ cup chianti
- 1 cup sour cream
- ½ cup brown sugar

Action

Soak the berries in chianti for an hour or so, and pour off the residue. Fold in sour cream until the berries are more or less evenly coated—until they're all involved with each other. Shake the brown sugar over the top and serve at room temperature.

Angst

Dear Reader,

I'm not the first to tell you that responsibility comes with knowledge. I have learned this mainly through food- because everything is about food, and because some foods represent a point of no return. Using garlic, balsamic vinegar, grinding your own coffee beans: these simple things re-create your standards, and you will have to live up to them forever. People you once respected will open a can of coffee and seem suddenly like tragic losers- and they are. Be careful of this recipe- it is irrevocable.

Irrevocable Dusted Ricotta

Food

- Powdered coffee
- Chocolate

- Ricotta cheese

Action

Grind the beans of the best coffee you can find as if you were making espresso. If you're up to it, put a tablet of bittersweet chocolate in your bean grinder. It could get gummy, so chill it first. This is really a test of your dedication to chocolate. Shake the powders together in a little bag, pour onto a clean surface, and roll rounds of the ricotta in the dust.

DREAM JOURNAL

The handsome guy who owns the vintage record shop
falls suddenly and madly in love with me. We have
a lunch made in heaven. And he says I can have any
ten CDs in his shop. The next day I go there to choose
them, and he tells me he realized over night that I
probably represent too much responsibility.
I ask if I can have five CDs then, and he says no.

Melon Ice: The Depression Litmus

Food

- 1 honeydew melon
- 1 cup sugar

- Mint leaves
- Splash gin or vodka

Action

There is no question that this dessert will make you feel like the richest person around. If you can eat this and think of something your life is lacking, then you haven't learned anything here; and we're almost at the end of the book.

Cut away the rind of the melon and slice into pieces. Boil them with the sugar for just a minute in a pan of enough water to keep the melon from scalding. Process this or use a blender until it's smooth, along with the mint leaves, which you add last and only for a split second. Freeze this for a little while, then take it out and process it again. Repeat this five or six times until it seems presentable. You can pour in the gin or vodka pretty much anytime along the way.

Dear Professor Angst,

I want to thank you soooooo much. I think it was your recommendation that got me the job at Mucha Mocha.

You've got to come for coffee (on me) and meet my partner Helmut, the coolest guy in the whole, complete entire world ever.

Yours,
Charlotte

Coffee to Reduce the Edge of Intolerable Company

Food

- 1 cup coffee, the way you like it

- Pinch ginger
- ½ cup port wine

Action

Heat these together and serve with a slice of lime.

PSYCHOLOGY, MEN & SOBBING

A NEW MAGAZINE ABOUT EVERYTHING FOR EVERYBODY

Dear Professor Angst,

Your submission - Women Who Cook Too Much - isn't really right for PMS.
Hope you'll try us again.

The Editors

Marsala Oranges for Women Who Cook Too Much

Food

- 1 orange, peeled, wedges separated and arranged on a plate
- Splash Marsala
- Sprinkle sugar

Action

If all of life were so simple.

Index